MANCHESTER

A Pictorial Hist

by

TED GRAY

Memories

ISBN: 1 899181 05 9

Published by   **Memories,** 222 Kings Road Manchester M16 0JT

Prepared by   **Northern Publishing Services**
28 Bedford Road
Firswood   M16 0JA
Tel: 061 862 9399

Written by   **Ted Gray**

©   **Ted Gray**

Design &
Layout by   *liff Hayes*

Printed by   **Manchester Free Press**
Longford Trading Estate
Thomas Street, Stretford
Manchester, M32 0JT
Tel: 061 864 4540

FRONT COVER: The *'Manchester Division'* in the Mersey Estuary.
(Photo B. & A. Fielden)

BACK COVER: Stern of the second *'Manchester Regiment'* (1947-68),
in 9 Dock, Salford, 1966.

COVER DESIGN: The Manchester Liners' funnel markings.

Other Books by Ted Gray:

- Salford Buses
- Manchester Buses

Tramways of Salford

Salford City Transport

Trafford Park Tramways

The Manchester Carriage and Tramways Company

100 Years of the Manchester Ship Canal

Greetings from Salford

Greetings from Eccles

- See inside back cover for other titles from Memorie

THE AUTHOR

TED GRAY is a local historian with special interest in transport history. Educated at Salford Grammar School and Westminster College, he entered the teaching profession in 1952, then studied in his spare time for a degree in Economic History at London University. He taught in Salford, Oldham, and Worsley; became Senior Lecturer in Education at Didsbury College, Manchester; and afterwards was Headteacher of Walkden High School.

An interest in ships began in childhood. Entrances to the Docks were guarded by Ship Canal police, but it was possible to catch fleeting glimpses of vessels at the end of No. 8 Dock. In Trafford Road, on the public side of the Dock Office, and conveniently located by the tram stop, the inner portion of one window was fitted with a hinged blackboard, on which a clerk chalked details of expected arrivals and departures that day. The names of the ships, their cargoes, and exotic-sounding far-away ports, made fascinating reading for a small boy. Nearby was a newsagent's shop, which displayed a selection of Charles Downs' ship photographs in a frame by the door. Downs must have had authority to wander at

Ted Gray at Salford Quays. In the background is the new Welland Lock, leading into Ontario Basin, the new name for the former No. 8 Dock.

will on Ship Canal territory, for he would photograph a ship, develop and print the film, and within a few hours postcards would be on sale for members of the crew to send home to their families. Purchased one at a time at a cost of only a few pence, these pictures formed the nucleus of a collection of views of the regular users of the Canal – Manchester Liners, Prince Liners, and the 'Pacific' ships of the Furness Withy Group. As a teenager, in a vain attempt to emulate Downs, the writer borrowed his father's old 'Box Brownie' camera to take snapshots near Barton. In adult life, when appointed to Ordsall Secondary School, he was delighted to find that his top-floor classroom enjoyed a splendid view over the perimeter wall into No. 7 Dock.

Boyhood interests eventually developed into more serious studies, and the author has since completed several publications on transport matters, including a centenary history of the Manchester Ship Canal.

ACKNOWLEDGEMENTS

The illustrations reproduced in this volume have been collected over a considerable period. The author is indebted to the Manchester Ship Canal Company for providing several photographs, and also for granting permits from time to time since 1950 for the author's own photographic excursions. Many of the earlier pictures are from the camera of the late Charles Downs. The illustrations are individually acknowledged where the photographer is known, and apologies are offered for any inadvertent omissions.

The author is grateful for the assistance provided by R. Alexander, formerly Public Relations Officer of Furness Withy; John Cooper of Norman Edwards Associates, Manchester; David Attenborough, Manchester; Warren Ayres of Fotoflite, Kent; Roy Mewha, Salford; Roy Jones, Denton; library staff at the Merseyside Maritime Museum; and officers of H.M.Customs & Excise, who granted access to shipping registers.

'*The Saga Of Manchester Liners*' by Robert B. Stoker, the third member of the Stoker family to have managed the Company, was published in 1985, and offers personal insight into the history and affairs of the shipping line. Similarly, '*Furness Withy, 1891-1991*' by David Burrell (World Ship Society, 1992) is a scholarly and comprehensive history of the Group and its subsidiaries. The author is indebted to both authors for much information included in this book. Various issues of the house journal, 'Manchester Liners News,' have provided many background details of the day-to-day working of the fleet.

INTRODUCTION

The Manchester Ship Canal, opened in 1894, was not an immediate success, even though, as an inducement to shippers, dues were not charged at first on through traffic. Many shipowners preferred to maintain their established services through traditional ports. They were not tempted to add a five or six-hour passage along a 36-mile canal to an untried inland port. Those with vested interests in Liverpool were concerned about the possible loss of trade and port dues, and therefore discouraged use of the Ship Canal. Calamities were forecast for ship-owners foolish enough to risk their vessels on the new waterway.

The 'Conference' system (rings of ship-owners) worked to keep services out of the canal. A new service from Manchester to the west coast of Africa offered carriage of goods at rates considerably cheaper than those payable via Liverpool, but the Conference members lowered their charges to drive away the competition, and induced customers to sign binding contracts. African steamers then reverted to Liverpool, with the consequent addition (for Manchester merchants) of railway and transfer charges. Another new service to Mediterranean ports was similarly halted when the established cartel cut rates for Manchester goods, an advantage which turned out to be only temporary when the old charges were re-imposed.

However, a number of north-eastern ship owners demonstrated their faith in the success of the Canal by purchasing land near Mode Wheel and forming the Manchester Ship Canal Pontoons & Dry Dock Company. Amongst the directors of that Company was George Renwick, of Newcastle, who later established the regular Fisher Renwick sailings between Manchester and London. A West Hartlepool line, Sivewright Bacon, transferred all its interests to Manchester. In 1894 Christopher Furness, of Furness Withy & Company, with extensive ship-building and ship-owning interests in the north-east, proposed a service to carry cotton goods between Manchester and India – the Manchester, Bombay & General Navigation Company. This, too, aroused the opposition of a 'Conference' ring, which, when faced by a combination of merchants determined to gain lower rates, felt obliged to compromise and buy out Furness's new company. However, the condition that the ships came to Manchester was retained, and as a result both Anchor and Clan Lines began regular sailings.

Furness investigated other possibilities, amongst which were a few trial sailings to Montreal in mid-1897. He recognised that if a Manchester-based Company was to succeed, local support was essential. Furness therefore offered to take a major shareholding in a Manchester shipping line on condition that Manchester business interests were prepared to invest. The Ship Canal Company, too, was most anxious for such a venture to succeed. Its representatives negotiated an annual subsidy from the Canadian Government, on the understanding that Canadian exports of grain and meat would be major cargoes. Support was enlisted from the Canadian Pacific Railway and American meat-packing interests. As a result, Manchester Liners Limited was formed in 1898.

As the largest shareholder, Sir Christopher Furness was elected Chairman, and arranged to manage the new Company from West Hartlepool until the necessary administrative structure had been established in Manchester. Robert Burdon Stoker, one of Furness's most trusted senior managers, was appointed as Managing Director. The Stoker family was destined to direct the operations of Manchester Liners over three generations, and the undoubted success of the enterprise proved a major factor in the fortunes of the Ship Canal.

Manchester Liners' services began with two second-hand ships purchased from the Elder Dempster Line in June 1898 for £60,000. They were the *Queensmore* and the *Parkmore*, immediately renamed *Manchester Enterprise* and *Manchester Trader*. Both ships, new in 1890, were eight years old, and well-known in the Canadian trade. The *Manchester Enterprise*, seen here with stalls erected on deck for the carriage of live cattle, had a short career with Manchester Liners, lasting only eighteen months. She had a reputation for rolling (even in dry dock, claimed one witness) and she leaked. In December 1898, on passage home to Manchester, she was towed into Queenstown with heavy weather damage, and on the 15th November 1899, bound for Montreal, she foundered in a gale. The ship was lost, but the crew members were rescued.

The *Parkmore* had been the first ship to bring grain in bulk to the new grain elevator on Trafford Wharf. As the *Manchester Trader* she lasted longer than her companion, though she, too, had a poor reputation – it was alleged that when blown by a strong headwind, she could travel faster going astern, than when powered by her engines going ahead! Nevertheless, she sailed for some 14 years on the North Atlantic, being sold in 1913 to a Norwegian company. Re-named *Ferdinand Melsom*, sold again and re-named *Kaupanger* in 1915, she met her end in the Mediterranean in December 1916 when torpedoed by a German U-boat.

The Company's first new ship, the *Manchester City*, was completed by Raylton Dixon & Co. at Middlesborough in 1898, the largest vessel built on the Tees at that time. She was fitted with telescopic masts and funnel to enable her to pass easily under bridges, but, even so, at 461 feet long, the *Manchester City* was so big that many doubted whether she could sail successfully along the Ship Canal. She was the largest meat ship of the period, with refrigerated space and additional accommodation for 700 live animals. On her maiden voyage from Canada, the passage along the Canal was accomplished smoothly, and cattle and sheep were discharged at the 'lairages' on Trafford Wharf. Reports of the successful passage of such a large ship did much to instil confidence in the Canal. It encouraged other shippers to use the Port of Manchester, and inspired Manchester Liners to order more new ships from north-east yards. From 1906 the *Manchester City* participated in the frozen meat traffic from the Argentine, remaining in service for 30 years until broken up at Stavanger, Norway, in 1929.

PHOTO: CHARLES DOWNS

MANCHESTER CORPORATION

Three new vessels were gained by taking over orders for ships already under construction for Furness Withy – the *Manchester City* at Raylton Dixon's yard and the *Manchester Port* and *Manchester Merchant* at Palmers' Ship-building, Jarrow. Orders were placed for four additional vessels, two from the Furness Withy yard at West Hartlepool (*Manchester Corporation, Manchester Commerce*) and two from Irvine's. Thus, by 1900, despite the loss of the *Manchester Enterprise*, the fleet had grown to a total of eight vessels. The services to Canadian ports were augmented with regular sailings to Boston, Philadelphia, and the southern cotton ports of New Orleans and Galveston. The Boer War led to a number of unusual voyages, when ships were requisitioned by the Government to act as troop transports or supply ships. The *Manchester Corporation* (here in Number 9 Dock in 1905), had made voyages to South Africa in her first year, carrying troops and horses. Three other Manchester ships were similarly involved for varying periods.

The *Manchester Importer* (1899), and her sister ship the *Manchester Shipper*, were products of Irvine's Shipyard at West Hartlepool. The *Manchester Importer* is seen about 1912 entering Mode Wheel locks inward-bound from Montreal. The tug is the MSC's *Eastham*. The second picture 'Bird's Eye View Of Manchester Docks,' is a commercial postcard dating from the 1920s. The main terminal docks lay in Salford, and the photograph was taken from the top of the Trafford Wharf grain elevator, looking in a north-easterly direction across to the Salford side. It shows the *Manchester Importer* high out of the water at the quay opposite, possibly laid up awaiting sale. In the foreground is a ship of the Prince Line. The *Importer* was sold to Greek owners in 1927, renamed *Alexandria*, and finally scrapped at Venice in 1933.

The *Manchester Shipper* (1900) had a similar life-span to her sister-ship, remaining in service until sold for breaking up in 1930. Headed by the tug *Eastham* (a regular worker for Manchester Liners), she is seen passing through Barton; and unloading at the head of 7 Dock, Salford.

MANCHESTER SHIPPER
UNLOADING -

PHOTO: SANKEY, BARROW

The **Manchester Port** was sold in 1900, but the expansion of the fleet continued, and in the period 1901-1904 another nine new ships were delivered.

Manchester Exchange	1901
Manchester Engineer	1902
Manchester Inventor	1902
Manchester Market	1902
Manchester Spinner	1903
Manchester Miller	1903
Manchester Port (II)	1904
Manchester Merchant (II)	1904
Manchester Mariner	1904

Sadly, the first *Manchester Merchant*, which from new in 1900 had been chartered for the Government's Boer War traffic for some 30 months, was lost in January 1903 as she approached the end of her first voyage for the Company. On passage from New Orleans to Manchester with a cargo of cotton, a serious fire was discovered. She ran for shelter in Dingle Bay on the west coast of Ireland, where she was scuttled in an attempt to put out the flames, and broke up in bad weather some days later. The *Manchester Market* was lost three months later, April 1903, when, outward-bound for Philadelphia, and sailing in thick fog off the south-east coast of Ireland, she was wrecked on the Tuskar Rock. Thus, in 1904 the fleet consisted of 14 ships which were to be the mainstay of the services for the next decade. The *Manchester Exchange* is seen moored by the No. 1 Grain Elevator, Trafford Wharf, discharging Canadian grain in 1921. The *Manchester Engineer*, lost during the 1914-18 War, is heavily-laden on passage down the Canal.

Manchester Merchant (II) was delivered in January 1904, and
replaced the ship of the same name which had been lost in 1903.
Seen discharging cargo at the head of 7 Dock, she remained in
service for some 30 years until sold for breaking up in 1933.

PHOTO: CHARLES DOWNS

The years 1902-1912 were a period of keen competition amongst shippers. Of the 14 ships in the fleet, 11 were engaged in the Canadian trade and three were deployed elsewhere. The *Manchester City*, by then fully insulated, created a record by carrying the largest consignment of frozen and chilled meat up to that time. She remained working from the River Plate, sailing to several British ports. Not until 1912 were further additions to the fleet contemplated. In 1911, prospects had brightened as a result of an agreement with three Canadian steamship companies for transhipment arrangements. These new plans enabled Manchester Liners to offer services via Montreal for through cargoes to Great Lakes ports. Subsequently, orders were placed for two new ships, and in 1912 the Northumberland Shipbuilding Company delivered the *Manchester Citizen*, which was followed by the *Manchester Civilian* from Irvine's. At the start of World War I, the *Manchester Civilian* was requisitioned as a supply ship, based in the South Atlantic around the Falkland Islands. When she returned in 1916, she carried supplies and equipment from Canada to troops in France. She is seen as fitted with mine-sweeping gear.

Manchester Liners suffered considerable losses during the First World War. In 1914 the *Manchester Commerce*, outward-bound for Montreal, was lost off north-west Ireland, the first merchant ship to be sunk by a mine. The *Manchester Engineer*, after being requisitioned by the Admiralty, was torpedoed in 1916, and in 1917-18 the Line lost no fewer than eight more ships, including four bought as hasty replace-ments for previous sinkings. The *Manchester Hero*, already building for Austrian Lloyd at the outbreak of war, was taken over by Manchester Liners and delivered in 1916. Seen here in the Mersey, she survived the first war, but, ironically, after sale to an Italian company, fell victim in the second war, when (as the *Capo Vita*) she was sunk by a British submarine in 1941.

The *Manchester Port* (II) of 1904 was another vessel to survive the First World War only to be sunk in the Second. She is seen (right) dressed overall, presumably for peace celebrations in 1918, but still carrying defensive armament mounted on the poop deck. In 1917 she had beaten off a submarine attack with gunfire. The second picture (below) shows her shortly before sale to a Hamburg company in 1925, when she was re-named *Vogesen.* She was lost after hitting a mine in 1940.

PHOTOS: CHARLES DOWNS

Two new ships, the *Manchester Brigade* and the *Manchester Division*, were completed at Irvine's shipyard in 1918. The *Manchester Division* gained instant fame when, on her maiden voyage from the West Hartlepool shipyard to join a convoy at Plymouth, she rammed and sank a German submarine in the North Sea. The *Manchester Brigade* is seen in the Mersey Estuary; and moored in 1935 at the head of No. 9 Dock, a traditional berth for Manchester Liners. The *Manchester Brigade* was sunk by a torpedo whilst sailing in convoy in 1940, but the *Manchester Division* remained in service until 1953.

Manchester Docks: No.9. Dock. AHC.1788.

◄ Manchester Liners had continued the sailings to Canada throughout the 1914-18 War, and, indeed, had joined in a service to Baltimore. In 1920 services to New Orleans were resumed, and the Baltimore sailings were extended to Norfolk, Virginia. To replace vessels lost in the war, the *Manchester Producer*, built in 1916 as the *Start Point*, was purchased from Furness Withy in 1921 and sailed for Manchester Liners for 19 years. In the Mersey estuary, approaching Eastham locks, her masts are telescoped ready for passage along the Ship Canal. Berthed in No. 9 Dock in 1934, the Harrison Line steamer *Dorelian* lies opposite. The *Manchester Producer* was sold to the Board of Trade in 1939, and as the *Botwey*, was torpedoed north-west of St. Kilda in July 1941.

◄ PHOTOS: CHARLES DOWNS/ STEWART BALE

PHOTO: CHARLES DOWNS

The second *Manchester Spinner* was another ship purchased from Furness Withy to replace lost tonnage. She had been built in 1918 as the *Grampian Range*, and joined Manchester Liners in 1921 along with the *Manchester Producer*. With the *Manchester Civilian*, the *Spinner* later became a regular carrier in the coal trade from Sydney, Cape Breton Island, Nova Scotia. In 1942, during the Second World War, the *Manchester Spinner* sailed with supplies to India, and on 7th June 1944, with a volunteer crew, she led a line of block-ships, sunk off the coast of Normandy to act as a breakwater whilst troops and stores were landed on the beaches. Inward-bound on the Ship Canal, she is arriving at Irlam Locks.

In 1922 Manchester Liners took delivery of a new turbine steamer, the **Manchester Regiment,** which, at 7930 gross tons, was the Company's biggest ship to date. Originally, it had been planned to have three such ships, but confidence in the profitability of North Atlantic services was undermined by subsidised competition from America and a developing trade recession. In addition, there were worries about the high cost of the new ships, and excessive fuel consumption. Consequently, only one vessel was purchased. The **Manchester Regiment's** record from the Mersey to Quebec was seven days nine hours. In 1925 her captain won the gold-headed cane traditionally awarded each Spring to the master of the first ship to break through the St. Lawrence ice to reach Montreal, a feat repeated by several Manchester Liners captains. No. 9 Dock, June 1934.

PHOTOS: CHARLES DOWNS/B. & A. FIELDEN

Two new ships were acquired in 1925, the *Manchester Commerce* (III) and the *Manchester Citizen* (II), both from the Furness - yard. However, in the same year, still troubled by the American subsidies on the North Atlantic routes, the Company sold the *Manchester Mariner, Port,* and *Exchange.* More disposals followed – the *Manchester Importer* in 1927; the *Corporation* and the *City* in 1929; and the *Shipper* in 1930. The *Manchester Commerce*, with masts telescoped, is navigating the Ship Canal. Her sister ship, the *Manchester Citizen*, is in the Mersey estuary.

Photo: B. & A. Fielden

S.S. MANCHESTER EXPORTER.

▲ When the refrigerated ship *Manchester City* was due for withdrawal, the Company purchased a half-share in the motorship *El Argentino* in order to continue its interest in the River Plate frozen meat trade. Likewise, so many ships from the North Atlantic run having been sold, the 1918-built *Rexmore* was acquired in 1929 from the Johnston Line (part of the Furness Withy group). The vessel was renamed *Manchester Exporter*, and remained in service with the Company until sold in 1947.

▶ In 1933, amid the great trade depression, several ships were laid up. The *Manchester Merchant* was sold for breaking up, and the *Manchester Civilian* was sold to Greek owners. The sailing programme for the 1933 'summer season' lists the six ships allocated to the Quebec and Montreal sailings that year.

Photo: Charles Downs

As prospects brightened, fleet replacements were commissioned. The third *Manchester Port* arrived in 1935, to be followed in 1937 by the second *Manchester City*, and in 1938 the *Manchester Progress*. These new arrivals made possible the sale of *Manchester Hero* and *Manchester Producer* in 1939. The new vessels were equipped with automatic stokers, and had greatly-improved accommodation for both passengers (12) and crew. The *Manchester City* was photographed at Eastham in August 1937, on arrival from the builders. At the outbreak of war in 1939 the *City* became first a mine-layer, and then a naval auxiliary ship, working in the Far East.

The *Manchester Regiment*, photographed passing through Mode Wheel Locks, became an early casualty of the war. Outward-bound in December 1939 with general cargo for St. John, New Brunswick, she was proceeding without lights when she was run down by the Pacific Steam Navigation's *Oropesa*, which had been detached from an east-bound convoy.

PHOTO: CHARLES DOWNS

In wartime, ships were painted battleship grey for camouflage purposes, and names were obliterated to make identification difficult for the enemy. However, when in port, names were sometimes displayed on boards hung from the side or bridge, in order that dock workers might load cargoes on the correct ship. The **Manchester Division** survived the war to remain in service until 1951.

In 1940 the third ship to bear the name *Manchester Merchant* was delivered, followed in 1941 by a third *Manchester Trader*, the last of the pre-war orders, and in 1943 by a second *Manchester Shipper*. Unhappily, enemy action resulted in losses. The *Manchester Brigade* was lost in 1940 when, sailing in convoy off Malin Head, Northern Ireland, she was struck by a torpedo from the U-137. The new *Manchester Merchant* and the *Manchester Citizen* were both lost in U boat attacks in 1943. Fortunately, two of the new ships survived to join five pre-war ships in resuming the weekly service to Canada. The *Manchester Trader* is seen in 1948 in the turning basin of the terminal docks at Salford, being swung by tug M.S.C. *Onward*. The *Manchester Shipper*, viewed through the deck clutter of another ship, is in No. 9 Dock, Salford. The *Shipper* was the first Manchester Liner to successfully navigate the St. Lawrence by means of radar equipment, an aid which was subsequently fitted to all vessels on that service.

In 1947 a new *Manchester Regiment* arrived. The Company, then with eight ships, instituted a programme to replace its war losses and renew the fleet. A new *Manchester Merchant*, the fourth ship of that name, was delivered from the Blythswood yard early in 1951. A full No. 9 Dock has the *Merchant* berthed left, opposite to the Strick Line's *Karaghistan*.

PHOTO: ELSAM, MANN & COOPER

PHOTO: STEWART BALE

In 1950 Manchester Liners placed an order with Cammell Laird, Birkenhead, for a new *Manchester Spinner*. The Company further decided to meet the demands of Canadian inland shippers by ordering two specially-designed ships of restricted size, small enough to navigate the canals and locks leading directly to Toronto and other Great Lakes ports.

Subsequently, on the 30th January 1952 a unique ceremony took place on the occasion of the dual launching of the new *Spinner* and the smaller *Manchester Pioneer*. The *Spinner* left the slipway first and was guided into the Mersey estuary, and the *Pioneer* followed, both to be towed into the fitting-out basin.

MANCHESTER EXPLORER

PHOTO: A. DUNCAN

A month after the delivery of the first '*laker*,' its sister ship, the ***Manchester Explorer,*** was ready. The numerous locks on the Lachine, Welland, and Soo Canals limited the size of ships able to reach the five Great Lakes beyond, but, with the St. Lawrence Seaway project evidently destined to become a reality, Manchester Liners wished to gain a foothold in the direct trade. The services offered by the small ships were so successful, that a third vessel, the ***Vigor*** (built 1948), was purchased from Norwegian owners in 1953 and re-named ***Manchester Prospector.*** In the winter months, when the ships were prevented by ice from reaching the Great Lakes, they were employed elsewhere, sometimes on charter.

◄ Another remarkable pioneering venture of the early 1950s was a summer service to Churchill, Manitoba, via Hudson Bay. These sailings were scheduled during the short ice-free season. In the first year, the associated Cairn Line's *Cairnavon* was used, but in the second season the service, greatly welcomed by grain importers, was carried out by the *Manchester Progress*.

▶ The *Manchester Mariner* of 1955 was built by Cammell Laird for the traditional services to Montreal and other east coast ocean ports. At this time, services had resumed to the southern United States ports of Charleston, Savannah, and Jacksonville.

As the services to the Great Lakes developed, two more small vessels were ordered, this time from the A. G. Weser shipyard at Bremen. Delivered in 1956, they were the first motorships owned by Manchester Liners. Engines and accommodation were at the stern, leaving as much space as possible for a large hold. Named *Manchester Vanguard* and *Manchester Venture*, they were chartered in the winter months by Yeoward Line, working in the fruit trade from the Canary Islands.

At the beginning of 1959 Manchester Liners owned 14 ships. In anticipation of the opening of the St. Lawrence Seaway, three more vessels were on order, two of which, built by Austin & Pickersgill at their Sunderland yard, were designed specially for the Seaway trade. They were the *Manchester Faith* and *Manchester Fame*. The *Manchester Faith* was the first ship to enter the Seaway on its official opening in 1959.

PHOTO: NORMAN EDWARDS ASSOCIATES

Larger vessels were now able to reach the Great Lakes ports, and so, inevitably, the five small *'lakers'* faced redundancy. The *Manchester Pioneer* was actually lengthened from 250 to 290 feet in Manchester Dry Docks, and subsequently made some of the most adventurous voyages ever undertaken by a Manchester Liner (Goose Bay, Labrador; Baffin Island; and remote spots on Hudson Bay, where cargoes were unloaded into barges by Eskimos) but all the small ships were sold by 1963. The *Pioneer* is seen as lengthened by Manchester Dry Docks in 1960. In this period, the familiar black hulls of Manchester Liners were painted light grey.

The third vessel delivered in 1959 was the *Manchester Miller*, built by Harland & Wolff at Belfast. At 9296 gross tons, she was the biggest ship yet owned by Manchester Liners. In 1970, after ten years service as a general cargo ship, she was returned to the shipyard to be converted into a cellular container ship, renamed *Manchester Quest*.

Services to ship grain in bulk from Duluth (Minnesota), at the head of Lake Superior in the heart of the North American continent, were offered as an experiment. The trials proving successful, the services were extended to include edible oils, for which cargo the **Manchester Commerce** was specially designed. Supplied in 1963 by Smith's Dock, Middlesborough, she was the fastest ship in the fleet at that time. The **Manchester City** (1964) and **Manchester Renown** (1964), were similar ships from the same builder. All three were sold in 1971, in the 'containerisation' period.

In the 1960s, the small Cairn Line, a member of the Furness Withy Group, had only three ships, which operated a service to Canada from the east coast ports of Britain. However, cargoes diminished somewhat, and in 1965 the three ships were chartered to Manchester Liners, being replaced on the east coast service by two smaller vessels, *Manchester Faith* and *Manchester Fame* (temporarily renamed *Cairnesk* and *Cairnglen*). The *Manchester Freighter* (ex-*Cairnforth*, 1959) and *Manchester Exporter* (ex-*Cairndhu*, 1952) remained with Manchester Liners until sold in 1969, but *Manchester Engineer* (ex-*Cairngowan*, 1952) reverted to her previous managers and name in 1966. The *Manchester Exporter*, moored near the end of 9 Dock, opposite Trafford Wharf, was photographed in 1967 during a three-month lay-up in a period of slack trade.

A 1964-65 extract from his Seaman's Record Book, shows that Roy Jones sailed on the last voyage of the 1935 *Manchester Port*, before transferring to the *Manchester Fame* and remaining with that ship during its temporary re-naming as *Cairnglen* when chartered to work for Cairn Line from South Shields, Grangemouth, and Leith. Note that the ship's Official Number, 300145, remains the same despite the change of name.

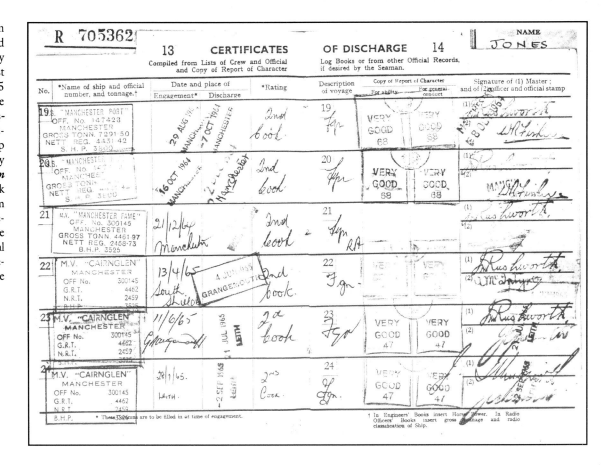

◄ By the mid-1960s Canadian ice-breakers were working to keep the St. Lawrence open in winter, so Manchester Liners took the opportunity to establish a year-round service. The new *Manchester Port* (1966) and *Manchester Progress* (1967) were specially strengthened to withstand the ice. They were also equipped with vertical tanks in which to carry lard from Chicago. At this date, Manchester Liners owned, or had on charter, no fewer than 20 ships sailing on the North Atlantic or the Great Lakes. The *Manchester Progress* was discharging 598 tons of lard at Runcorn in 1968.

PHOTO: ELSAM, MANN & COOPER

Labour problems, escalating shore costs, and American competition led the Company to investigate the sort of cargoes which could be usefully carried in containers. Consequently, because of the associated operations required for container traffic, Manchester Liners diversified into a group of companies, covering road haulage, warehousing, engineering, and (with the acquisition of Morrell Mills in 1968) facilities for container and ship repair work. [In 1974 Manchester Liners also acquired Manchester Dry Docks.] The Company took over the Prince Line's Mediterranean services in 1968, and absorbed the Cairn Line's North Atlantic routes. Orders were placed with Smith's Dock Company, Middlesborough, for three cellular container ships, the first ordered by a British shipping line. At the same time, designs were drawn up for a major investment programme in the provision of suitable terminals at Montreal and Manchester. The *Manchester Challenge* made the first sailing for Montreal in November 1968.

◄ The *Manchester Concorde* was Manchester Liners' third large container ship, delivered from Smith's Dockyard in 1969. The new vessels were designed for a rapid passage (6½ days Manchester-Montreal), a quick turn-round, and the shortest possible time in port – two days, as against ten or more for a conventional ship. For the year-round service, an *'ice-knife'* was fitted around the rudder, offering protection if the ships had to go astern into the St. Lawrence ice. Note the "crow's nest" look-out post in the bows. At the outset, the maximum capacity was 500 containers, because originally, in view of North Atlantic weather conditions, it had been decided to carry all containers below deck. The size of the vessels was limited by the 600-feet-long by 65-feet-wide locks on the Ship Canal. The Manchester container-base was established near the end of No. 9 Dock, where were stacked some of the 10,000 containers ordered for the start of the new service.

PHOTO: NORMAN EDWARDS ASSOCIATES

▶ The container vessel *Manchester Concorde* breaking through the winter ice of the St. Lawrence River on her way to Montreal.

◀ Containerisation changed the face of the shipping scene. Most traditional vessels were sold off as new container ships were commissioned, but the *Manchester Quest* was a 1970 conversion of the 1959 *Manchester Miller*, and similarly, the *Manchester Concept* was a 1971 conversion of the 1967 *Manchester Progress*. The *Quest* is seen by the container terminal with tanker *Peakdale H* alongside. The prow of *Manchester Merit* may be seen far left. Manchester Liners moved from the St. Ann's Square headquarters to a new building within the dock estate in 1969. 'Manchester Liners House' (now 'Furness House') was shaped like the bridge of a ship, and offered accommodation for the increased numbers of administrative staff. A new Customs House was constructed at the rear. In 1970 Furness Withy, which since 1898 had always had a substantial interest in the Company, increased its shareholding from 42% to 56%, making Manchester Liners a subsidiary.

PHOTO: NORMAN EDWARDS ASSOCIATES

The *Manchester Merit* was launched in Spain in 1970 as the *Catalina del Mar*, and was purchased for the Mediterranean services. She was a smaller container vessel, named at first *Manchester Merito*. After a spell in Canada sailing between Montreal and Chicago, she became the first British container ship to work in the Mediterranean, collecting cargo for North America to be shipped via the United Kingdom. On charter to a Bermudan company from 1972 as the *Fortuna*, she was sold in 1975 to the Chelwood Shipping Company and renamed *Kathleen*. Oddly, she became a Manchester Liner once again in 1979 when she was chartered for the Great Lakes feeder services. A 1970 photograph shows her with red hull, being swung in the turning basin at Salford by the tug *Undine*. The Salford Quays redevelopment programme has commemorated the former links with the Great Lakes by naming the old docks *Ontario Basin*, *Huron Basin*, and *Erie Basin*. There is even a *Welland Lock*. Inexplicably, however, the former turning basin appears on Project Office maps as *The Harbour*.

PHOTO: NORMAN EDWARDS ASSOCIATES

Frontier was another small vessel acquired in 1972 from Spain and intended for the Med–iterranean services. With red hull and displaying the Manchester Liners' logo on the bow, she had not yet been re–named *Manchester Frontier* when this picture was taken.

By the end of 1971 the large container ships were operating on the North Atlantic services, with two feeder vessels based at Montreal. Orders were placed with British shipyards for two vessels of 4490 tons for delivery in 1973, and two more large 12,000 tonners for 1974.

The two 1973 deliveries were the *Manchester Vigour* and her sister ship *Manchester Zeal*, small general purpose ships, built at Appledore. They were used both on Mediterranean and Atlantic services.

FOTOFLITE, KENT

Two new large container ships arrived at a time of uncertainty in 1974, when the Eurocanadian Company (Cast) was attempting to buy up Manchester Liners' shares and integrate operations. Furness countered by increasing its holding in Manchester Liners to nearly 62%. The Monopolies and Mergers Committee ruled that mergers between Eurocanadian and Manchester Liners, or between Eurocanadian and Furness Withy, should not be permitted. Eurocanadian then arranged for its sailings from Antwerp to call at Liverpool, with the aim of reducing the traffic carried by Manchester Liners. When this ploy failed, the Antwerp operations were serviced by feeder ships from British

ports. The two new ships, *Manchester Reward* and *Manchester Renown*, were immediately placed on charter to the China Navigation Company, not returning until 1978, when it was decided to operate the North Atlantic service from Liverpool and to sell the 1968 vessels, *Manchester Challenge* and *Manchester Courage*. In the meantime, Manchester Liners themselves chartered a number of vessels for varying periods as traffic demanded. The *Manchester Reward*, on passage through the English Channel, carries some containers on the hatch tops, the original decision on the inadvisability of deck cargo having been rescinded.

Sister ship to the 1977 *Manchester Vanguard*, the second *Manchester Venture* is seen at the container terminal at Greenock. The later and larger container ships had a more angular appearance, accentuated by the containers on deck, and lacked the graceful lines of earlier traditional vessels.

Photo: Norman Edwards Associates

In 1980 the Furness Group was purchased by Orient Overseas Holdings, controlled by C. Y. Tung of Hong Kong. Assurances were given that the Group would continue trading, unaffected by the take-over. Indeed, consolidation of the Furness Group's interests continued, with the acquisition of Eurocanadian's shares in Manchester Liners, making it a wholly-owned subsidiary. The chartering of smaller ships continued in the early 1980s. In 1981-82 the *City Of Ipswich*, was chartered from the Ellerman Line and temporarily renamed *Manchester Fulmar*.

The small container vessel *Manchester Clipper*, of only 1595 gross tons, was chartered from a German company in 1980-83. Though renamed, and carrying Manchester Liners containers, she was displaying her previous operator's paint style and funnel markings when photographed leaving Grand Harbour, Valletta, Malta.

Cut-throat competition and fewer cargoes on the North Atlantic services eventually forced action to avoid losses. In 1981, each hoping to keep a share of the market, the three main providers of the Canadian services, Manchester Liners, Dart Container Line (Canada), and Canadian Pacific, instituted a co-ordinated weekly service to Montreal from the containerbase at Felixstowe, calling also at Hamburg, Antwerp, and Le Havre as required. It was agreed to operate this service with four large ships, each company providing one, and sharing in a fourth. Manchester Liners' contribution was the second *Manchester Challenge* (ex-*Dart America*), a vessel transferred from the Dart Container Line. Too large to have navigated the Ship Canal, it is seen in the Dover Straits. Some 12 years after the container service had first begun, this ship delivered the two-millionth container to Montreal.

B Y 1985 only three vessels remained with the *'Manchester'* title. The C. Y. Tung Group was troubled by high running costs and depressed freight rates. Furness Withy funds, which might otherwise have been reinvested, were diverted to Hong Kong to help rescue the Group. In 1988 all branches of the container business were absorbed into the Orient Overseas Container Line, and Manchester Liners lost its shipping interests. After an existence of 90 years, Manchester Liners disappeared.

In 1983, traffic on the upper reaches of the Manchester Ship Canal had dwindled to such an extent that Manchester Liners announced their intention to work the remaining services from Ellesmere Port. The **Manchester Crown** (ex-*Crown Prince* of 1979, which had been transferred from the Prince Line in 1983) is loading containers at Ellesmere Port. The ship was sold in 1985.

FLEET LIST

Vessels are listed in order of building, acquisition, or charter. Several names were used more than once. In such cases, the number in brackets after the name, e.g. *Manchester Merchant* (2), indicates whether this was the first, second, third, or fourth ship to carry that name. In the 1970s and '80s, vessels on charter were given a *'Manchester'* name temporarily, usually reverting to original name on return to the owners. For full details of re-namings, see R. B. Stoker's *'The Saga Of Manchester Liners.'*

The funnel marking adopted by Manchester Liners was red with a black top and a black band. The house flag was white, with a red oval in the centre on which appeared the letters ML in white.

Abbreviations: GRT = Gross Registered Tonnage   b.u.= broken up   cc = cellular container ship

Name		GRT	Built	Acquired	Sold	Notes
Manchester Enterprise (ex-*Queensmore*)		3878	1890	1898	—	Foundered 14/11/1899
Manchester Trader (ex-*Parkmore*)	(1)	3318	1890	1898	1913	
Manchester City	(1)	7696	1898	—	—	b.u. 1929
Manchester Port	(1)	5658	1899	—	1900	
Manchester Corporation		5400	1899	—	—	b.u. 1929
Manchester Commerce	(1)	5397	1899	—	—	Mined & sunk 1914
Manchester Importer		4028	1899	—	1927	
Manchester Merchant	(1)	5657	1900	—	—	Scuttled on fire 1903
Manchester Shipper	(1)	4076	1900	—	—	b.u. 1930
Manchester Exchange		4091	1901	—	1925	
Manchester Engineer	(1)	4302	1902	—	—	Sunk by U44 27/3/1916
Manchester Inventor	(1)	4247	1902	—	—	Sunk by U57 18/1/1917
Manchester Market		4901	1902	—	—	Wrecked 26/4/1903

Manchester Exchange, 1901-1925

Manchester Shipper (I), 1900-1930

Manchester Spinner (I), 1903-1918

Manchester Mariner (I), 1904-1925

Name		GRT	Built	Acquired	Sold	Notes
Manchester Spinner	(1)	4227	1903	—	—	Sunk by U27 22/1/1918
Manchester Miller	(1)	4234	1903	—	—	Sunk by U66 5/6/1917
Manchester Merchant	(2)	4152	1904	—	—	b.u. 1933
Manchester Port	(2)	4093	1904	—	1925	
Manchester Mariner	(1)	4106	1904	—	1925	Mined but saved 1917
Manchester Citizen	(1)	4251	1912	—	—	Sunk by U70 26/4/1917
Manchester Civilian		4706	1913	1933	—	
Manchester Hero		5738	1916	1937	—	
Manchester Trader (ex-Archenbloe)	(2)	3938	1902	1916	—	Sunk by U65 4/6/1917
Manchester Commerce (ex-King)	(2)	4144	1906	1916	—	Sunk by U39 29/7/1917
Manchester Engineer (ex-Nation/Craigvar)	(2)	4415	1905	1917	—	Sunk by UC16 16/8/1917
Manchester Inventor (ex-Celtic King)	(2)	4112	1907	1917	—	Sunk by U94 30/7/1917

(The above four ships were purchased to replace war losses, and three were reported to have been given the same names as lost ships in order to confuse the enemy. Sadly, all four were themselves lost in mid-1917.)

Name		GRT	Built	Acquired	Sold	Notes
Manchester Brigade		6021	1918	—	—	Sunk by U137 26/9/1940
Manchester Division		6027	1918	—	—	b.u. 1953
Manchester Producer (ex-Start Point)		6576	1916	1921	1939	
Manchester Spinner (ex-Grampian Range)	(2)	4767	1918	1921	—	Normandy blockship 1944
Manchester Regiment	(1)	7930	1922	—	—	Lost in collision 1939

Name		GRT	Built	Acquired	Sold	Notes
Manchester Commerce	(3)	5342	1925	—	1952	—
Manchester Citizen	(2)	5328	1925	—	—	Sunk by U508 9/7/1943
Manchester Exporter (ex-Rexmore)	(1)	5277	1918	1929	1947	—
El Argentino		9501	1928	—	1934	Half-share with British & Argentine Co. in this refrigerated motorship
Manchester Port	(3)	7291	1935	—	—	b.u. 1964
Manchester City	(2)	7296	1937	—	—	b.u. 1964
Manchester Progress	(1)	7346	1938	—	—	b.u. 1966
Manchester Merchant	(3)	7264	1940	—	—	Sunk by U628 25/2/1943
Manchester Trader	(3)	7363	1941	—	—	b.u. 1963
Manchester Shipper	(2)	7881	1943	—	—	b.u. 1969
Manchester Regiment	(2)	7638	1947	—	1968	—
Manchester Merchant	(4)	7651	1951	—	1967	—
Manchester Pioneer		1805	1952	—	1963	* Small vessels for direct services to Great Lakes
Manchester Explorer		1805	1952	—	1963	*
Manchester Spinner	(3)	7814	1952	—	1968	—
Manchester Prospector (ex-Vigor)		1400	1948	1953	1960	*
Manchester Mariner	(2)	7580	1955	—	1968	—
Manchester Vanguard	(1)	1662	1956	—	1963	First vessel to enter St. Lawrence Seaway, 1959
Manchester Venture	(1)	1662	1956	—	1961	—
Manchester Faith	(1)	4459	1959	—	1970	—

Manchester Port (III), 1935-1964

Manchester Regiment (II), 1947-1968

Manchester Fame, 1959-1970

Manchester Renown (I), 1964-1971

Name		GRT	Built	Acquired	Sold	Notes
Manchester Fame		4462	1959	—	1970	—
Manchester Miller (*Manchester Quest*)	(2)	9296	1959	—	—	Converted to cc 1970 & renamed, b.u. 1976
Manchester Trader (*ex-Western Prince*)	(4)	5758	1955	1963	—	Chartered from Prince Line 1963-69
Manchester Commerce	(4)	8724	1963	—	1971	
Manchester City	(3)	8734	1964	—	1971	
Manchester Renown	(1)	8742	1964	—	1971	
Manchester Freighter (*ex-Cairnforth*)		8105	1959	1965	1969	Taken over from Cairn Line Ltd.
Manchester Exporter (*ex-Cairndhu*)	(2)	7506	1952	1965	1969	Taken over from Cairn Line Ltd.
Manchester Engineer (*ex-Cairngowan*)	(3)	7503	1952	1965	—	Taken over from Cairn Line; returned 1966
Manchester Port	(4)	8938	1966	—	1971	
Manchester Progress (*Manchester Concept*)	(2)	8176	1967	—	1973	Converted to cc 1971, & renamed
Manchester Challenge	(1)	12039	1968	—	1979	cc.
Manchester Courage		12039	1968	—	1979	cc.
Manchester Concorde		12039	1969	—	1982	cc.
Manchester Merit		3414	1970	—	1975	cc.
Manchester Crusade		12039	1971	—	1982	cc.
Manchester Mercurio		1997	1971	—	—	cc. Chartered 1971-80
Manchester Rapido		1997	1971	—	—	cc. Chartered 1971-78

Name		GRT	Built	Acquired	Sold	Notes
Manchester Frontier		3621	1972	—	1979	cc. On charter
Manchester Vigour		5310	1973	—	1980	cc.
Manchester Zeal		5310	1973	—	1981	cc.
Lindo		6411	1972	—	—	cc. Chartered 1973 Great Lakes feeder service
Manchester Faith	(2)	1421	1974	—	—	cc. Chartered 1974-83
Manchester Shipper	(3)	500	1973	—	—	Chartered 1974-75
Manchester Renown	(2)	12577	1974	—	1982	cc. On charter to China as *Asian Renown*
Manchester Reward		12577	1974	—	1982	& *Asian Reward* 1974-78
Manchester Fulmar	(1)	2524	1974	—	—	cc. Chartered 1974-79
Manchester Falcon		999	1975	—	—	cc. Chartered 1975-76
Manchester Vanguard	(2)	17385	1977	—	—	cc. Chartered 1979-81
Manchester Venture		17385	1977	—	—	cc. Chartered 1977-80
Manchester Clipper		1595	1980	—	—	cc. Chartered 1980-83
Manchester Eagle		965	1972	—	—	cc. Chartered 1981-82
Manchester Fulmar	(2)	1599	1979	—	—	cc. Chartered 1981-83
Manchester Challenge (ex-Dart America)	(2)	30817	1970	1981	—	cc. Transferred from Dart Container Line
Manchester Crown (ex-Crown Prince)		1599	1979	1983	1985	cc. Transferred from Prince Line 1983
Manchester Trader	(5)	1999	1977	—	—	cc. Chartered 1984-85
Manchester Faith	(3)	1599	1971	—	—	cc. Chartered 1985
Manchester City	(4)	3598	1978	—	—	cc. Chartered 1985
Manchester Trader	(6)	3978	1978	—	—	cc. Chartered 1985